Over or Under

by Wiley Blevins

Raintree is an imprint of Capstone Global Library Limited, a company incorporated in England and Wales having its registered office at 264 Banbury Road, Oxford, OX2 7DY – Registered company number: 6695582

www.raintree.co.uk
myorders@raintree.co.uk

Text © Capstone Global Library Limited 2020
The moral rights of the proprietor have been asserted.

All rights reserved. No part of this publication may be reproduced in any form or by any means (including photocopying or storing it in any medium by electronic means and whether or not transiently or incidentally to some other use of this publication) without the written permission of the copyright owner, except in accordance with the provisions of the Copyright, Designs and Patents Act 1988 or under the terms of a licence issued by the Copyright Licensing Agency, Saffron House, 6–10 Kirby Street, London EC1N 8TS (www.cla.co.uk). Applications for the copyright owner's written permission should be addressed to the publisher.

Edited by Erika Shores
Designed by Elyse White
Picture research by Tracy Cummins
Production by Laura Manthe
Originated by Capstone Global Library Limited
Printed and bound in India

ISBN 978 1 4747 6873 3 (hardback)
ISBN 978 1 4747 6888 7 (paperback)

British Library Cataloguing in Publication Data
A full catalogue record for this book is available from the British Library.

Acknowledgements
Shutterstock: Don Mammoser, 5, Franny Constantina, Cover, Katerina Izotova Art Lab, Design Element, Lienka, 13, photolinc, Design Element, SelimBT, 9, studio lallka, 11, TaOuu, 17, TreasureGalore, 19, 21, Vixit, 7, woodHunt, 15.

Every effort has been made to contact copyright holders of material reproduced in this book. Any omissions will be rectified in subsequent printings if notice is given to the publisher.

All the internet addresses (URLs) given in this book were valid at the time of going to press. However, due to the dynamic nature of the internet, some addresses may have changed, or sites may have changed or ceased to exist since publication. While the author and publisher regret any inconvenience this may cause readers, no responsibility for any such changes can be accepted by either the author or the publisher.

London Borough of Enfield	
91200000699036	
Askews & Holts	16-Sep-2020
J428.1 JUNIOR NON-FI	
ENSOUT	

Contents

Where is it?....................4

In the desert..................6

In the forest..................12

Over and under the water.....18

Glossary....................22
Find out more...............23
Answers to questions........23
Comprehension questions....24
Index.......................24

Where is it?

What do you see?

It is a bear cub. The bear cub climbs over the log. Soft grass is under the log.

In the desert

The desert is hot and dry.

The camels walk over

the hot sand.

How many camels can

you see?

The owl flies over the desert. The sand is under the owl. The owl has long wings.

The goats walk over the rocks. They are under a blue sky. The desert is far below.

In the forest

The snake hides under a log. It waits for prey to come near.

A lady is riding her horse in the forest. The horse jumps over the log. The stirrups are under her boots.

The butterfly hangs under a leaf. The butterfly is very colourful.
What colour is it?

Over and under the water

The bridge crosses over the pond. The pond is under the bridge. There are plants all around the pond.

The fish swim under the water. The fish are red and orange. How many fish are there?

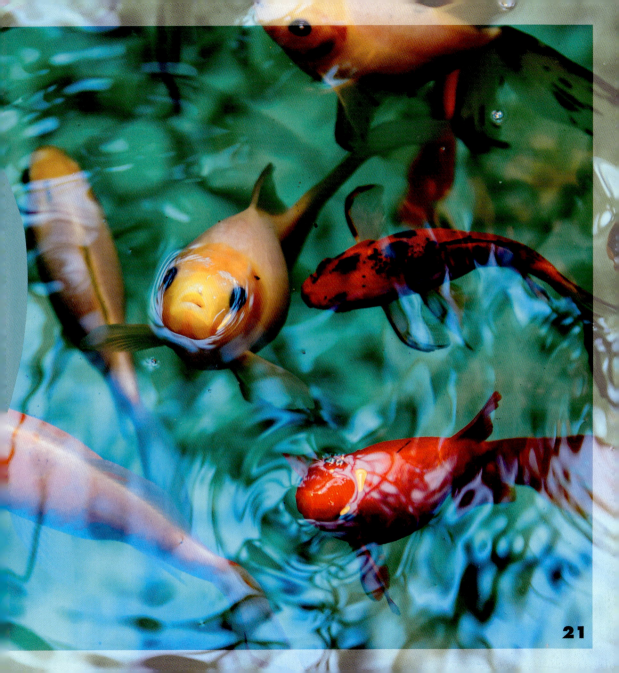

Glossary

cub a young bear

desert a place where very little rain falls

hooves hard covering on the foot of an animal. Goats, horses and donkeys all have hooves.

log a part of a tree that has fallen down

prey an animal that is eaten by another animal

stirrups metal loops that a rider puts his or her feet into

Find out more

Eddie and Ellie's Opposites at the Farm, Rebecca Rissman (Raintree, 2013)

Opposites! (Look & Learn), National Geographic Kids (National Geographic Kids, 2012)

Opposites (Board Book), Penny West (Raintree, 2014)

Website

www.bbc.com/bitesize/clips/zy26sbk
This BBC Bitesize video introduces the use of words to describe their location.

Answers to questions

Here are the answers to the questions in the book: Page 6: there are nine camels; Page 16: the butterfly is yellow, orange, blue and black; Page 18: there are six fish.

Comprehension questions

1. What is the weather like in the desert?

2. What do you think might live in a pond?

Index

bear cub 4
bridge 18
butterfly 16
camels 6
desert 6, 10
fish 20
goats 10
grass 4
horse 14
lady 14

leaf 16
log 12, 14
owl 8
plants 18
pond 18
rocks 10, 14
sand 6, 8
snake 12
water 18, 20